✓firesong

firesong

ANNE POWELL

STEELE ROBERTS LTD
AOTEAROA NEW ZEALAND

*In memory of my parents
Mary and Pat Powell*

Cover photo: Judith Schumacher
Design: Lynn Peck

Published by Steele Roberts Ltd

Box 9321 • Wellington • Aotearoa New Zealand
Phone (04) 499 0044 • Fax (04) 499 0056
email rwsteele@actrix.gen.nz

isbn 1-877228-14-1

March 1999

Contents

Introduction

Last year I made a pilgrimage to The Lyell, that once-flourishing, now ghost town, deep in the Buller Gorge. My maternal great-grandparents, Luigi Carmine from the north of Italy and Catherine Concannon from the west coast of Ireland, created their first home there in 1879. He, a cobbler in that mining town, and she, the mother of nine children, musician and gatherer of people.

There I experienced a deep connection with these ancestors. On the day of my visit, on the white stones and the wet green bush of The Lyell, I met them. And I know, beyond any doubt at all, that before I was ever born I am in this land, these rivers, this bush, this light. For ages past, I am the speck of gold awaiting the hour of my birth.

This experience of spirited connection centres me. It is a focal point out of which I write. This book expresses an identity flowing from a sense of place, relationship to this place, its people and context.

Events on my journey which deepen this sense of place and connection are many, as are the people who have been signposts for me on the way.

In New Plymouth, between the mountain and the sea, I grew up in a family bound together by books and music, vege gardens with enough freesias and zinnias and poppies to make a difference, and a faith that does. Our extended family deepened that awareness of word and music through family concerts, stories, humour, song and practical care for others struggling because of lack of resources.

Later, as a young teacher, I remember being criticised by the inspectors for my emphasis on creative writing and dance. I believe that everyone possesses a deep well of potential creativity. It helps when others encourage us to let down the bucket into the well and believe in our gifts. My parents did that. My brother and sisters continue to do that for me. There's a mutuality there. Some of these poems hold our family story.

In my twenties, I joined the Cenacle Sisters, an international congregation of women which originated in France in 1826. Through the Cenacle, my sense of place was challenged and expanded to embrace a sense of the spirit. I believe in the possibility of direct encounter with a personal God who welcomes discovery in all places, events and people. As a Cenacle Sister I have had plentiful opportunities to companion people on their inner journeys, where the context is often one of search for meaning, purpose and wholeness. Some of these poems reflect those journeys and play beams of light on the searching.

Through friendships I feel the tug and challenge of love. I know and receive the commitment that steadies friendships over years. Some of these poems flow out of relationships. Others begin simply in my own imagining. Some of these poems tell of death ~ a death that strikes while the rest of us shudder and try to go on living.

Through the Cenacle, especially in my recent years in the role of regional leader, I have had opportunities for a great deal of exposure to other places and cultures. There, my instinct is to take off my shoes, in radical openness to the new.

In 1996, when I had completed six years in that leadership role, the thing I most wanted to do was write. Several years previously Joy Cowley read some stories I'd written for my nieces and nephews as Christmas presents. Joy said, "Go to Whitireia Polytech's writing course." At that time work demands prevented me from doing so. But in 1997 I was able to join several weeks of the writing module part-time. At the end of those weeks Rachel McAlpine said to me, "Go and publish."

What began as a desire to continue writing for children grew into a rediscovery of myself as writer, reluctant to bear the name 'poet.' What began as writing to present a folio of original poems for assessment grew into a fire burning in me.

Through 1998 I wrote whenever I could find time and intentional solitude for the work.

This first collection of poems stirs questions:

- *What is our sense of place?*
- *What is our relationship with the land?*
- *What is our sense of spirit?*
- *What is our sense of connectedness?*
- *What is our sense of purpose?*
- *What is destructive around us?*
- *What is life-giving for us?*

There's a mysticism of place I am discovering. There's the context, increasingly fractured and troubled, of people's lives. There's the call of the Spirit ~ the wild, white swan.

THE POETRY LIBRARY

I hope these poems shine enough light and sense of connection to make a difference. In risking asking the questions and living into the answers, I believe we discover a stronger sense of identity and authentic spirituality as people privileged to live in the place where

no land
at all
at all
breaks the fall
and rise of waves
once they leave Antarctica.

Acknowledgements

My gratitude to my family and to the Cenacle Sisters, co-workers and friends who were part of the journey of this book. Thanks also to Rachel McAlpine for editing, my sister Judith Schumacher for the cover photo, Roger Steele for commitment, and Veronica Williams for proof-reading.

Thanks to the editors of the following where some of these poems first appeared: *Tui Motu, Wel-Com, Australian Journal of Feminist Studies in Religion – Women – Church.*

Anne Powell
MARCH 1999

place

Shapes

Taranaki is my mountain.
Waiwhakaiho is my river.
Ngamotu is my standing place.

I grew
up there
under the leisurely eyes of cows.

Once when I was little
I cut my eyebrows off
with scissors.
"My God!" yelled Mum
"they'll never grow again!"

Back then
a daring thing to do
under the eye of the mountain
watchful
like God
behind a cloud.

Back beach

If you go down
to the back beach south
of Ngamotu
you will find that
the sand is black.

If you lie down
on the back black beach
it irons away
your worries.

If you dig down
in the black back beach
you will find oil
and China.

Karanga at Korma Road

Karanga hangs in the afternoon air
haunting the land
and the trees
and the place where clothes rest light
upon our spines.

E kui,
wrapped in the black rug,
sacredness becomes you.

Up north

There was a time when
kauri grew chewing gum if
you mixed it with milk of puwha

spitting in your hands you'd
take your spear, spade and
pikau bag and
dig deep in the cold

swamp for gold
sold in your dreams
for a woman you could carve
into a wife.

Coromandel

The sensual curl
and lick of wave
on limb
and land

and you

making hay at home
while the sun shone
on me
and the kids.

Down under

"What's a creek?" he asks.
"Don't you know? Everyone knows
what a creek is."
"Well, tell me," he asks.
So I lead him with "Come on!" and
away we go down the rough road and over
the shaky fence into Honeyfield's paddock.

"There's the creek," I point.
"Where? I can't see anything," he pouts.
"You have to get in it," I shout.
Together,

we fall on the grass
and pull off shoes and socks
so our feet bounce on the spring of the grass.

Next thing, we're in it. "Is this a creek?" he calls.
But I don't hear because
I am there
already stealing my way up the creek
loving its coolness
relishing its squish
tickling its tadpoles with my oh so white toes
the creek's dark water my domain.

Boy from Ethiopia
hot espresso pools for eyes
trembles a toe
down under
the cool water.

No land at all

When you stand and
face due south
at Cook Strait
did you know that no land
at all
at all

breaks the fall
and rise of waves
once they leave Antarctica?

Sequin sequence

I
Sequin stars sparkle
in the black vault.

II
Even when they tumble,
there's the frail outline of where
they were sewn.

III
Sequined sky
I wonder why
night is black.
You fill its cracks
with shine.

IV
Sequins don't shake
in the stately saraband.

V
I can't stand sequins
so I'll dance.

Thinking the land

You would be forgiven for
thinking the land
a lizard lying in wait
for the lick of the sea.

You would be forgiven for
thinking the Spit
a bird pecking scraps from the sea
at the tip of the south.

You would be forgiven for
thinking the land
a voice as you lie in the lee
of the hill near the smell of the sea.

But the plastic and glass,
aluminium and tin that you fling
does not lie easily
on the land which will rise

quaking with rage
chanting its own dirge:

> *Oh sun, moon and stars!*
> *Taupo! Waitangi!*
> *Gather the cloak*
> *loose like silk flowing.*
> *Greed provokes this bleed*
> *and it is no small thing.*

people

Perspectives

It all depends on your point of view, I said. Now
I'm a cloud watcher from way back.
Let me loose on a bright morning,
tri-colour scarf wrapped round
my neck and I move
to the clouds' rhythm.

Even a kiteless sky stirs me.
When the wind's too strong
I long to go out and
see clouds shredded and shunted
south to Kaikoura ~
the whales' table
and river stones
mattresses and maps of Ireland.

At the window he drums
on the lip of wood
eyes glazed as an ice pond.
It's all in the mind, he says

while I,
cloudwatcher,
surely see a mask float by
with holes for eyes.

Buttoned up

Sources close to the president
and the prime minister
talked themselves out
for a day off.

They met on a headland
in a hot air balloon.
Forgetting the craft of making silence
their talk caused the balloon to rise
in the sky like a gold lollipop
high for the parched tongue of the sun.

Interviewed after, they said the drift
most leisurely
most interesting
taught us nothing
we didn't know already

except this ~
that the earth's a button
and ourselves so small
we could run through the hole in the middle.

Reading space

I sit alongside a man of middle age.
One of us wears black Doc Martens and
a speckled woolly hat and
a wine-red cravat and
sunglasses rimmed with fluorescent lime and
fine white ankle socks and
school grey short shorts and
a green V-neck jersey from The Warehouse.

One of us reads
"From Chorus Line to Tinsel Town"
with lips pleading for pleasure
and the toes try tip tap
trapped in the black shoes.

Out the window I see
the side of the Gallery
and five steel pipes screwed
to the wall.
This one reader rivets me.

Tom's secret life

Tom spends Saturdays weeding
the plot ~
silver beet, broccoli, leeks
the stuff of quiche.

Tom's wife orders through the open window
Bring me some parsley.

Tom bends
wanting to grow invisible
wanting to catch parsley in the act
of curling on its thin legs.

Four girls and the piano man

for John, Marie, Joan, and Judith

When he was little
he lived in a piano
scaling higher than Hillary
or hammering.

He gave us ponds of wild white swans
while we washed
dressed
and ate our breakfast.

Later
he came out of the piano.

Turn left

First you go left
at Blagdon Road
then circle the roundabout
into Haunui Street.
That's a long one.

You go straight
along it till you come to the dairy
with the flowers outside in buckets
(they're yellow and blue usually, you say).

Keep going past the dairy
and then turn
left into Waka.
From there you can see the sunset
and follow the stars.

Blue ribbons

Imagine wind like a hairdresser
combing the clouds
in the salon of sky.

Say *delphinium*.
A word worth writing
like wildblood
ribbons
and Pacific rose.

Six letter word

Winter holds the cold
in six letters
wrapped round my neck
like a rough scarf
choking autumn.

Winter holds the cold
in six letters
making ice
for whizzing round the rink.

Winter holds the cold
outside
while I hold you in bed

warm.

Freesias and cardigans

Hurry on spring!
On your wings
the breath of freesias
in the Ming vases of emperors
and the jars and bar bottles of old women
flinging off worries like cardigans.

Spring bulbs
in dark ground
are threatening
resurrection.

Soul song

Girl
take care
not to bare your soul
to every Tom, Dick or Harry
who wants to marry

you.

When the phone rings
take down your dulcimer
and sing.

Cream honey

"Where are you going to, my pretty maid?"
"I'm going a-milking, sir," she said.

Down the track of mud
and the creek in flood
she flicks her stick
in the black air.

"Where are you going to, my pretty maid?"
"I'm going a-milking, sir," she said.

Her gumboots squelch and suck
in the muck
till she reaches the shed
and feels sounds surround her.

The tails of cows
are metronomes now
to the music relaxing them and her,
colouring the shed and her dream
with the cream light of
honey moon disappearing.

"Where are you going to, my pretty maid?"
"I'm going a-milking, sir," she said.

Woman refuge

Your bruises flare like revenge
like the hollow of a paua shell
kicked over

you lie
open to sky
pleading rain or seaweed
to shield you.

Later,
you crawl crab-like down
to the sea.

Hints for middle years

You want to get
to where you're going
even if you don't have a map

or a torch
or a long piece of rope
for emergencies
let alone a Band-aid.

The thing is to do the journey.

Enjoy wherever you pass
be it city
or shore line
or paddock
or people.

And tune your breathing
to the rhythm of soul.

Rhythm and roar

She met
a man who
questioned her
"If you were knocked down
by a bus today
how many poems
would die with you?"

She knew
she'd caught
a few.

That night her pen
is needle threaded with fire
is diviner's rod trembling
to the tug of water.

Next morning
there's an empty page on her kitchen table
there's cup and cutlery and unclean
plates on the bench
there's her husband rattling keys and
locked in pages of words written
by other people.

Not her.
She's heard her own words now
in the room of drenching
unquenching
rhythm and roar of
water and fire.

88 Vivian Street

Nodding by the fire
she smells her grandmother
sees her high-stepping among
ribbons of flames
tastes the comfort of the bread
and the dripping
and the sipping of tea
hears the rattling of peg bag
and bones grown old.

Knows the loneliness of a single willow
bending by the water
nodding by the fire.

All the time

Madelena carries the fish
in the green shopping bag
with cherry handles
up Cuba Street to
Webb where smoke tars her
kitchen walls and
hangs in the curtains.

With her back to no one
slips the fish into the sink
begins to bathe it
counts off each scale like gold
holds the limp body
anoints it with juice of a half lemon
and all the time in the world.

Some people

Some people know what it's like to wait
for hip replacements
or the bus in the drizzle
or a job

for the phone to ring
or benefit day
or enough white, sliced bread

for TB
or the rent collector
or glue ear to skip the house

for the next quick fix
slow foxtrot
or fight to stop

or love without bruises

and others don't.

In the heat

Nana stands in the heat
of her kitchen
wearing her pinny
print from the past
spooning Anzac biscuits
onto the tray.
Licking the last

and tasting Gallipoli
and thinking she hears
an opening
and calling
"Is that you, dear?"

But
Pop's still
down on the beach.

True blue

The morning after
when the sky smiled blue
a small plane flew over us
breathing a trail of smoke
which wrote *I'm sorry*
in the sky.

We looked at each other
then made stories about the pilot and
the person on the ground and
how the smoke's trail resembled
a tamed dragon.

But looking around
we saw only us.

She cannot bear this parting

She cannot bear this parting from her lover
who sails the seas of the world
in his boat.

She cannot bear this parting from her lover
as standing at the window watching
the white, night moon stir
in its darkening bed.

She cannot bear this parting from her lover
while chained by the moon at her window,
elsewhere, over some sparkling, rhythmic sea
the sun warms the loins of her lover.

Anniversary

Something surprises her
seizes her by the shoulders and shakes
loose a memory

and she's in that room
at the bedside
where the Styx licks and slaps at the door
like a hungry dingo.

Next thing
there's water sneaking
up on her black shoes
then it's up to the metal legs
of the hospital bed and she wonders

will her chair float
away bearing her as a barge
And now the water drenches the overhang of sheets
and she can't stand it
as a rush of water heavier
than the flooded Whanganui
knocks the feet from under her
and she wants to shake
her fist skywards
but she's drowning
and can barely breathe.

She notices
how now her hands move
like drugged trout
in this world of under water.

Time slows.
Stops.

River flows.

She knows
her mother,
once fearful swimmer goes
gracefully on the dark water
to the other side.

Home
on land
she stands looking
into the old photo
then goes
to hang out the washing
with the memory
to dry.

The circle

There is strength and safety
in the circle of women
in this room of honour
and round bellies
with sapphires for shoulders
amethysts for arms
lazuli for legs
and diamonds for dancing.

We are resilience of rocks
at the ancient centre of earth.

Sand patterns at Waitarere

Walking it out.
Walking it out.
I stamp and shout for miles on the empty beach
at Waitarere.

Your face
surprises me in a sand pattern
till the tide runs away with you
and I'm left with a hollow
sand pit of grief.

If

in memory of Margaret Clapham

If I had the money
Margaret,
I'd buy all the white roses in the world
and lie them face up to the sky
over you.

If I had the money
Margaret,
I'd buy all the clocks in the world
and halt time the day before you said
good-bye.

If I had the money
Margaret,
I'd buy God
and scream "You sod!" as earth
thuds on your coffin.

Pillow feather dreaming

I dreamed the two of us had finished
work and we took
our books and briefcases
to the beach.

We stand in the cool sand.
We wait for the float plane.
We climb in.

It whirrs above the water
like a bird up
and blind, hits the fine lines
taut across the Strait.

I wake to the pluck
of pillow feathers
the place your head nested
empty.

Death takes a holiday

13 August 1998
the *Bay City Reporter*
noted no deaths
from Aids.

Balloons held their breath and danced
high and round as the sun.
Bones made music
for thin-legged people to polka.

Families and friends drew breath and rainbows.
Quiltmakers lay fabrics and needles on the grass
having neither name nor tear
to embroider.

Instead they bought fine wine
bread to toast the tremulous
and brave
and death
who went on holiday.

three moons

skylark soars. high song
rests on the small of the back
of the moon.

moon wedge of lemon cheesecake
on the navy plate of sky
waiting.

cold moon on Awanui
cemetery.
mum and dad still in their tomb.

For your sake

The rain is riding
the back of the wind

The rain is hair
falling like silver

You love that wet-bush
smell of rain

For your sake, I will
grow my hair
long and silver
as rain

spirit

Horizons

Morning star
let there be light.

Between the leaves
let there be light.

Children's faces
let there be light.

On the horizon
let there be light.

Arc of rainbow
let there be light.

Candle at window
let there be light.

Dancing harp

We are the music.
We are the dance.
We ring the puriri
with the rhythm of feet.
Our fingers are playing
the unseen harp of the wind.

Here

Over cups of tea and coffee
the sacred becomes gathered warmth.

In low-fenced backyards and playgrounds
the sacred chatters and laughs.

On black sand beaches and stretching seas
the sacred shines.

Under cool ferns and green puriri
the sacred is uncovered.

In conflicts and misunderstandings
the sacred waits to be revealed.

On barefoot journeys of pilgrims
walks the sacred.

The pot of the world simmers with the sacred.
Take off the lid!

The learning tree

I draw on strength
from rising moon.
I draw on strength
from Mary's womb.

I draw on strength
from tumbling waves.
I draw on strength
from One who saves.

I draw on strength
from kauri tree.
I draw on strength
and learn to be.

Like a koru

I am a listener
hearing
the split of silence
at Huka Falls.

I am a singer
making
music on the wind
in the tussocks.

I am a woman
awaiting
the rise of yeast
and the sound of bread growing.

I am a traveller
opening
like a koru
my ear.

Going deeper

Go down
    down
    down
to the place in you
where fire and silence dwell ~

the place of power.

Go down
    down
    down
to that pool in you
of weedless water ~

the place of knowing.

Go down
    down
    down
the moss bright path
to your Grandmother's house ~

the place of song.

Go down
    down
    down
to the last strawberry ~

freshness of God.

Cosmic breathing

I breathe in
I am land
I breathe out
I am listening

I breathe in
I am river
I breathe out
I am flowing

I breathe in
I am kauri
I breathe out
I am strong

I breathe in
I am rain
I breathe out
I am refreshed

I breathe in
I am rock
I breathe out
I am centred

Aotearoa litany

Green of fern	*refresh us*
Feathers of kereru	*warm us*
Rocks of Moeraki	*encircle us*
Waters of Taupo	*bathe us*
Dive of gannet	*focus us*
Arc of rainbow	*protect us*
Stars of Southern Cross	*guide us*

Goodness

Goodness has *oo* inside it.
It can catch my breath and whisk me away.
The *oo* can open me to "aha" moments ~
points of stillness, holy drama
or ordinariness
when the God in Go(o)dness leaps into the world
again and again.

The rhythm of goodness
beats at the heart of the door of the world.
The rhythm of goodness

smiles
moves
graces places
and I move with its easy air.

Blessing

May the soft light
at the end of the day
heal you.

May the purr of the sea
on the shells of the beach
heal you.

May the dance of the wind
on the grass of the dunes
heal you.

May the Maker of water
and air and fire
heal you
who walk the earth.

Temples and tea

Gandhi,
we're in quandary
for the land of temples
and tea
suddenly trembles

and the hands of the poor
reach for roti

and the sacred cow turns
now
into mushroom.

The West Bank

There's a tree
standing sentry-straight
out of the concrete
reminding me of home
and Rita Angus' painting
of the sole tree
bare and daring
nakedness.

This tree stands
erect in a West Bank yard.
Branches shiver with gun-cold metal
killing time against the trunk.

Rocks and pearls

I sit on a rock
feet in the Sea of Galilee
where thoughts and images swirl
old and fresh as this sea
around me.

Like hen
or healer
like rock
or pearl
like grain
or gate
like sheep
or tree
like fire
or fountain
like baker
or vine
like a woman
searching for that coin.

My feet in the Sea of Galilee
feel the images flow
clear as rocks below water.

My feet in the Sea of Galilee
feel the presence
of One who washes
soothes, cools
creates and comes.

Joy, justice and ginger

Advent
Arrival
We wait for the flavours and focus
of Christ-coming ~
peacefulness and joy
justice-making, love
and red-wrapped boxes of ginger.

Advent
Arrival
We wait for the silent feet
of camels
and the clatter of Kaimanawa horses
startled on the Desert Road
of summer holidays.

Advent
Arrival
We wait for the gate to open
urging us
to step into the story
and the mystery
that calms and troubles the world.

Dream rising

Souks awaken.
And oh!
their sounds grow round and round

in thin alleys
where smells of tamarind and cinnamon
and almonds
seep into clothes.
Till in my dreams
it seems
I am woman of Jerusalem.

By Damascus Gate
an old Arab
hawks eggs and breads
from a box on a bicycle
his face ravined
with loss of land.
Till in my dreams
it seems
I am a place to stand.

The tomb guard
a man
upright and grand
as a piano.
His ivory hands
hurry people along.
Till in my dreams
it seems
I am a song
bright in the breast of a lark
rising.

---

souk   outdoor, often covered market,
        especially in North Africa and Middle East

All my stars

Woman of the Upper Room,
what did you tell them
of your boy
dead too soon?

That he was mobbed
and robbed by bandits
for enriching others?

That he was stoned
and broken
for mending lives?

Woman of the Upper Room,
what did you tell them
of your boy
dead too soon?

A lump as big as the earth
quakes your soul.
They've killed my sun
my moon and all my stars.

The travellers (Luke 8:1-4)

We are the travelling women.
Our names are lost
but the cost
of companioning Jesus
is not.

We are the lepers and widows
outcasts and bleeders
prayers and dreamers
who dared.

We are the bakers and servants
dancers and weavers
gossips, believers
who chose to be chosen.

Our names are lost like blood
in a red sea.
But the sound of our voice
is pulse to the pilgrim heart.

ॐ

OTHER STEELE ROBERTS POETRY

* *Montana Award winner*

K

If that the heavens do not their visible spirits
Send quickly down to tame these vilde offences,
It will come,
Humanity must perforce prey on itself,
Like monsters of the deep.
   (*King Lear*, IV.ii.46–50)